MUFFIN BOOK

Ocean Spray Fresh Cranberry Muffins

(Makes 12 - 14 Muffins)

1 punnet (227g/8oz) Fresh Ocean Spray Cranberries
140g (5oz) sugar
25g (1oz) butter or margarine
1 egg
125ml (4fl.oz) milk
227g (8oz) plain flour
1 heaped teaspoon baking powder
1 pinch salt

Pre-heat oven to 180°C, 350°F or Gas mark 4. Coarsely chop cranberries. In a bowl cream together sugar and butter. Add egg a little at a time and beat after each addition. In another bowl sift together flour, baking powder and salt. Add alternatively with milk to the creamed sugar mixture. Stir in chopped cranberries. Spoon into 12-14 paper cake cases - use two per muffin to help maintain shape. Bake for 30-40 mins or until golden brown and springy to the touch.

Other books in the Penguin Pocket Series

THE AUSTRALIAN CALORIE COUNTER
THE AUSTRALIAN EASY SPELLER
AUSTRALIAN GARDENING CALENDAR
BEST EVER IDEAS FOR CHILDREN'S PARTIES
CASSEROLES FOR FAMILY AND FRIENDS
CHAIRING AND RUNNING MEETINGS
CHESS MADE EASY
CHOOSING A NAME FOR YOUR BABY
CHOOSING AUSTRALIAN WINES
THE COMPACT GUIDE TO WRITING LETTERS
FAMILY FIRST AID
GABRIEL GATÉ'S FAST PASTA
GABRIEL GATÉ'S FAVOURITE FAST RECIPES
GABRIEL GATÉ'S ONE-DISH DINNERS
GOOD FOOD FOR BABIES AND TODDLERS
HOW TO MAKE OVER 200 COCKTAILS
HOW TO PLAY MAH JONG
JULIE STAFFORD'S JUICING BOOK
MICROWAVE MEALS IN MINUTES
MICROWAVE TIPS AND TECHNIQUES
THE PENGUIN POCKET BOOK OF QUOTATIONS
PLAYING CASINO GAMES TO WIN
THE POCKET AUSSIE FACT BOOK
REMOVING STAINS
SPEAKING IN PUBLIC
TRAINING YOUR MEMORY
USING YOUR NOODLES
WEDDING ETIQUETTE
YOUR NEW BABY

THE POCKET MUFFIN BOOK

Syd Pemberton

PENGUIN BOOKS

Penguin Books Australia Ltd
487 Maroondah Highway, PO Box 257
Ringwood, Victoria 3134, Australia
Penguin Books Ltd
Harmondsworth, Middlesex, England
Viking Penguin, A Division of Penguin Books USA Inc.
375 Hudson Street, New York, New York 10014, USA
Penguin Books Canada Limited
10 Alcorn Avenue, Toronto, Ontario, Canada M4V 3B2
Penguin Books (NZ) Ltd
Cnr Rosedale and Airborne Roads, Albany, Auckland, New Zealand

First published by Penguin Books Australia 1998

3 5 7 9 10 8 6 4 2

Designed by Ellie Exarchos, Penguin Design Studio
Illustrated by Michelle Ryan
Typeset in 10/13 pt Apollo by Post Pre-press Group, Brisbane
Printed and bound in Australia by Australian Print Group,
Maryborough, Victoria

National Library of Australia
Cataloguing-in-Publication data:

Pemberton, Syd.
The pocket muffin book.

ISBN 0 14 026851 0.

1. Muffins. I. Title.

641.815

CONTENTS

MARVELLOUS MUFFINS!

Muffins are so fast and easy to prepare that they can be served up for breakfast without any need to rise before dawn, whizzed up to add to a lunch box as a tasty sweet or savoury snack, or prepared for a last-minute afternoon tea. And they make a glamorous dessert just by adding ice-cream, fresh fruit or a delicious sweet sauce. Because of the speed with which muffins can be made, they can be put together and cooked just before you need to serve them. Watch them disappear before you can get them out of the tray!

Muffins are made by a very simple 'fast-mix' technique that uses a wide range of ingredients, many of which you may already have in your store cupboard. Savoury muffins are just as tasty as the more traditional sweet variety and can be a scrumptious addition to any lunch or dinner menu – try them with soup, a cheese platter or a casserole. Savoury muffins made in a mini-muffin tray are ideal to serve with drinks, on their own or with a dip.

The great thing about muffins is that once you have mastered the measuring, mixing and baking, you can try your own refinements! Add your favourite ingredients and make up your own recipes – this is a *great* way to teach children how to cook.

While muffins straight from the oven are hard to beat, they do not have to be served warm – some are just as delicious cold with butter or jam. Muffins can also be frozen successfully and they reheat easily in a microwave or standard oven.

It was a lot of fun developing and testing all the muffin recipes for this book. I thank all my hard-working critical tasters, each of whose response was invariably 'Mmmm, yummy!'

HOW TO USE THIS BOOK

The Equipment

The equipment you will need to make a basic muffin recipe includes things you are likely to already have in the cupboard:

- muffin tray
- measuring spoons
- standard metric measuring cups
- kitchen scales
- two (or sometimes three) mixing bowls
- a fork or balloon whisk
- two spoons

One bowl is used to mix the dry ingredients and the

other the wet ingredients (occasionally a third is used to prepare a topping). The fork or whisk blends the liquids, while one of the spoons mixes the wet ingredients into the dry. The other spoon is used to push the muffin batter off the mixing spoon into the muffin tray holes.

There are three basic muffin tray sizes, and the cooking times vary depending on the size of the tin you use.

- **mini**
  25 ml (1 tablespoon plus 1 teaspoon) capacity
  Baking time: 10–15 minutes
- **medium**
  80 ml (⅓ cup) capacity
  Baking time: 25–30 minutes
- **large** (Texas-style or jumbo)
  180 ml (¾ cup) capacity
  Baking time: 35–40 minutes

The recipes in this book are all based on a medium (⅓ cup) muffin tray, which makes twelve muffins that take around twenty-five minutes to cook. Most mixtures featured here will make about six of the large muffins and thirty-six mini muffins. Fill the muffin holes about two-thirds full for the best results when cooking.

The Ingredients

Most kitchen store cupboards will usually carry enough ingredients needed to whip up a batch of muffins at short notice. All you need is:

- flour (plain or self-raising, unbleached or wholemeal)
- sugar (soft light-brown, dark-brown or castor sugar, for example)
- an egg or two
- butter or oil (canola or vegetable oil, for example)
- liquid (often milk or buttermilk, or perhaps a fruit juice or yoghurt)
- and flavourings (chocolate, orange zest, coconut, dried fruit, cheese, mustard – and so on and so on)

I especially love using buttermilk when making muffins as it produces a lighter texture. Now available from supermarkets, it is low-fat milk that has had a culture added to it which creates a unique, slightly tangy flavour. (Originally, buttermilk was the residue left after butter was churned.) Plain milk can be substituted easily for buttermilk, however.

The Method

There are only three steps to making muffins:

1. *measure*
2. *mix*
3. *and bake.*

The most important thing to remember when making muffins is to be careful not to overmix the batter. It should be a little lumpy and the flour just lightly moistened (not at all like a smooth, well-mixed cake batter). Light of hand and light on speed! If you overmix the batter, the muffins will be tough rather than light and springy.

When preparing the muffin tray for baking make sure to grease it well – a pastry brush dipped in oil is good for this. Sweet muffins can sometimes be harder to remove from the tin, so let them sit for a minute before turning them out onto a wire rack to cool. Special care should be taken when turning out filled muffins: it is best to leave them for 4–5 minutes to cool before turning them out. And be careful eating hot, filled muffins: the filling can be like molten lava!

Freezing and Reheating

Most muffins can be frozen successfully for up to three months if packed carefully in an airtight container. They reheat wonderfully easily in a microwave or conventional oven and do not lose their 'oven-fresh' texture or taste.

To reheat frozen muffins in a conventional oven, preheat the oven to 160°C with a baking tray in it. Wrap each muffin in foil, then place them on the baking tray and cook for about fifteen minutes or longer, depending on the size of the muffins, until warm enough to eat.

Defrosting and reheating in the microwave is easy: as a rough guide, cook two frozen muffins on high for twenty seconds.

SWEET FAMILY FAVOURITES

Almond, Orange and Raisin Muffins

¼ cup raisins
hot water
2 cups unbleached self-raising flour
½ cup soft light-brown sugar
½ teaspoon ground cinnamon
1 tablespoon grated orange zest
¼ cup ground almonds
2 eggs
¼ cup buttermilk
¾ cup canola oil
1 tablespoon dark rum
1 teaspoon vanilla essence

Soak the raisins in a little hot water for 20 minutes, then drain. Preheat the oven to 180°C and lightly grease a muffin tray. Mix the flour, light-brown sugar, cinnamon, orange zest and ground almonds in a bowl. In a separate bowl, lightly whisk the eggs with the buttermilk, canola oil, rum and vanilla essence, then stir in the raisins. Pour the wet ingredients into the flour mixture and mix lightly until just combined. Spoon the batter into the prepared muffin tray.

Bake for 25–30 minutes or until the muffins spring back when lightly pressed. Remove the muffins from the oven and turn them out onto a wire rack to cool.

Apple and Pecan Muffins

2 cups unbleached self-raising flour
¼ cup soft light-brown sugar
1 cup pecan nuts, roughly chopped
2 cups peeled and finely grated Granny Smith apple
1 teaspoon ground cinnamon
1 teaspoon ground nutmeg
1 egg
1 cup buttermilk
¼ cup canola oil
1 teaspoon vanilla essence

Preheat the oven to 180°C and lightly grease a muffin tray. Mix the flour, light-brown sugar, pecans and spices in a bowl, then fold in the grated apple. In a separate bowl, lightly whisk the egg with the buttermilk, canola oil and vanilla essence. Pour the wet ingredients into the flour mixture and mix lightly until just combined. Spoon the batter into the prepared muffin tray.

Bake for 25–30 minutes or until the muffins

spring back when lightly pressed. Remove the muffins from the oven and turn them out onto a wire rack to cool.

FRESH NUTS ARE BEST KEPT IN THE REFRIGERATOR OR FREEZER IN AN AIRTIGHT CONTAINER – THEY CAN BECOME RANCID QUICKLY OTHERWISE.

Banana Chocolate Muffins

2 cups unbleached self-raising flour
¼ cup sifted cocoa powder
½ cup castor sugar
½ cup walnuts, chopped
1 egg
1 cup buttermilk
1 cup mashed banana
⅓ cup canola oil
1 teaspoon vanilla essence

Preheat the oven to 180°C and lightly grease a muffin tray. Mix the flour, castor sugar and cocoa powder in a bowl, then stir in the walnuts. In a separate bowl, lightly whisk the egg with the buttermilk, canola oil, vanilla essence and banana. Pour the wet ingredients into the flour mixture and mix lightly until just combined. Spoon the batter into the prepared muffin tray.

Bake for 25–30 minutes or until the muffins spring back when lightly pressed. Remove the muffins from the oven and turn them out onto a wire rack to cool.

Banana and Walnut Muffins

2 cups unbleached self-raising flour
½ cup soft light-brown sugar
½ teaspoon ground cinnamon
1 cup walnuts, chopped
1 egg
1 cup buttermilk
⅓ cup canola oil
1 cup mashed banana

Preheat the oven to 180°C and lightly grease a muffin tray. Mix the flour, light-brown sugar, cinnamon and walnuts in a bowl. In a separate bowl, lightly whisk the egg with the buttermilk, canola oil and mashed banana. Pour the wet ingredients into the flour mixture and mix lightly until just combined. Spoon the batter into the prepared muffin tray.

Bake for 25–30 minutes or until the muffins spring back when lightly pressed. Remove the muffins from the oven and turn them out onto a wire rack to cool.

Blackberry and Apple Muffins

1 cup unbleached self-raising flour
1 cup wholemeal self-raising flour
½ cup soft light-brown sugar
200 g blackberries
1 cup finely chopped dried apple
1 egg
1 cup buttermilk
80 g butter, melted

Preheat the oven to 180°C and lightly grease a muffin tray. Mix the flours and light-brown sugar in a bowl, then stir in the dried apple and blackberries. In a separate bowl, lightly whisk the egg with the buttermilk and melted butter. Pour the wet ingredients into the flour mixture and mix lightly until just combined. Spoon the batter into the prepared muffin tray.

Bake for 25–30 minutes or until the muffins spring back when lightly pressed. Remove the muffins from the oven and turn them out onto a wire rack to cool.

Carrot, Pecan and Sultana Muffins

2 cups unbleached self-raising flour
⅓ cup soft light-brown sugar
400 g carrots, peeled and finely grated
1 cup pecan nuts, roughly chopped
½ cup sultanas
2 eggs
¼ cup buttermilk
½ cup canola oil
¼ cup fresh orange juice

Preheat the oven to 180°C and lightly grease a muffin tray. Mix the flour, light-brown sugar, carrot, nuts and sultanas in a bowl. In a separate bowl, lightly whisk the eggs with the buttermilk, canola oil and orange juice. Pour the wet ingredients into the flour mixture and mix lightly until just combined. Spoon the batter into the prepared muffin tray.

Bake for 20–25 minutes or until the muffins spring back when lightly pressed. Remove the muffins from the oven and turn them out onto a wire rack to cool.

Cherry Coconut Muffins

1½ cups unbleached self-raising flour
½ cup castor sugar
½ cup desiccated coconut
1 cup glacé cherries
2 eggs
1 cup buttermilk
80 g butter, melted
2 tablespoons shredded coconut

Preheat the oven to 180°C and lightly grease a muffin tray. Mix the flour, castor sugar and desiccated coconut in a bowl, then stir in the glacé cherries. In a separate bowl, lightly whisk the eggs with the buttermilk and butter. Pour the wet ingredients into the flour mixture and mix lightly until just combined. Spoon the batter into the prepared muffin tray, then press a little shredded coconut onto each muffin.

Bake for 25–30 minutes or until the muffins spring back when lightly pressed. Remove the muffins from the oven and turn them out onto a wire rack to cool.

Chocolate Blueberry Muffins

2 cups unbleached self-raising flour
½ cup soft light-brown sugar
¼ cup sifted cocoa powder
150 g fresh blueberries
2 eggs
1 cup buttermilk
¼ cup canola oil

Preheat the oven to 180°C and lightly grease a muffin tray. Mix the flour, light-brown sugar, cocoa powder and blueberries in a bowl. In a separate bowl, lightly whisk the eggs with the buttermilk and canola oil. Pour the wet ingredients into the flour mixture and mix lightly until just combined. Spoon the batter into the prepared muffin tray.

Bake for 25–30 minutes or until the muffins spring back when lightly pressed. Remove the muffins from the oven and turn them out onto a wire rack to cool.

Date, Coffee and Walnut Muffins

2 cups unbleached self-raising flour
1 tablespoon cocoa powder
½ cup soft light-brown sugar
1 cup walnuts, chopped
¾ cup roughly chopped dates
2 eggs
½ cup buttermilk
½ cup canola oil
¼ cup strong black coffee
¼ cup sour cream

Preheat the oven to 180°C and lightly grease a muffin tray. Mix the flour, cocoa powder, light-brown sugar, walnuts and dates in a bowl. In a separate bowl, lightly whisk the eggs with the buttermilk, canola oil, coffee and sour cream. Pour the wet ingredients into the flour mixture and mix lightly until just combined. Spoon the batter into the prepared muffin tray.

Bake for 25–30 minutes or until the muffins

spring back when lightly pressed. Remove the muffins from the oven and turn them out onto a wire rack to cool.

Lemon and Ginger Muffins

2 cups unbleached self-raising flour
⅓ cup soft light-brown sugar
2 tablespoons grated lemon zest
100 g roughly chopped glacé ginger
2 eggs
1 cup buttermilk
½ cup canola oil

Preheat the oven to 180°C and lightly grease a muffin tray. Mix the flour, light-brown sugar, lemon zest and glacé ginger in a bowl. In a separate bowl, lightly whisk the eggs with the buttermilk and canola oil. Pour the wet ingredients into the flour mixture and mix lightly until just combined. Spoon the batter into the prepared muffin tray.

Bake for 25–30 minutes or until the muffins spring back when lightly pressed. Remove the muffins from the oven and turn them out onto a wire rack to cool.

Lemon Poppyseed Muffins

2 cups unbleached plain flour
1 tablespoon baking powder
⅓ cup castor sugar
2 tablespoons poppyseeds
1 egg
1 cup buttermilk
120 g butter, melted
grated zest of 1 lemon

TOPPING
juice of 1 lemon
¼ cup castor sugar

Preheat the oven to 180°C and lightly grease a muffin tray. Mix the flour, baking powder, castor sugar and poppyseeds in a bowl. In a separate bowl, lightly whisk the egg with the buttermilk, melted butter and lemon zest. Pour the wet ingredients into the flour mixture and mix lightly until just combined. Spoon the batter into the prepared muffin tray.

Bake for 20–25 minutes or until the muffins spring back when lightly pressed. Remove the muffins from the oven and turn them out onto a wire rack.

To make the topping, mix the lemon juice and sugar and brush this over the muffins while they are still hot.

Morello Cherry Jam Muffins

2 cups unbleached self-raising flour
¼ cup castor sugar
1 teaspoon grated lemon zest
1 egg
1 cup plain yoghurt
1 teaspoon vanilla essence
60 g butter, melted
¼ cup morello cherry jam

Preheat the oven to 180°C and lightly grease a muffin tray. Mix the flour, castor sugar and lemon zest in a bowl. In a separate bowl, lightly whisk the egg with the yoghurt, vanilla essence and melted butter. Pour the wet ingredients into the flour mixture and mix lightly until just combined. Spoon half the batter into the prepared muffin tray, then add 1 teaspoon jam to each muffin. Spoon in the remaining batter.

Bake for 25–30 minutes or until the muffins spring back when lightly pressed. Remove the muffins from the oven and turn them out onto a wire rack to cool.

WHEN STORING DRIED FRUIT, ADD A PIECE OF LEMON ZEST OR A BAY LEAF TO THE JAR TO KEEP IT FRESH AND TO DETER WEEVILS.

Nutty Chocolate Ripple Muffins

2 cups unbleached self-raising flour
⅓ cup castor sugar
1 egg
½ cup milk
80 g butter, melted

FILLING
20 g dark chocolate, finely grated
20 g softened butter
¼ cup soft light-brown sugar
2 teaspoons unbleached plain flour
½ teaspoon ground cinnamon
1 tablespoon finely chopped macadamia nuts

Preheat the oven to 180°C and lightly grease a muffin tray. To make the filling, put all the ingredients into a bowl, then rub the butter through with your fingers to make crumbs. Mix the flour and castor sugar in another bowl. In a separate bowl again, lightly whisk the egg with the milk and melted butter. Pour the wet ingredients into the flour mixture and mix lightly until just combined. Spoon half the batter into the prepared muffin tray, then add a little filling to each muffin. Spoon in the remaining batter.

Bake for 25–30 minutes or until the muffins spring back when lightly pressed. Remove the muffins from the oven and turn them out onto a wire rack to cool.

Old-fashioned Gingerbread Muffins

2 cups unbleached plain flour
½ teaspoon baking powder
¼ teaspoon bicarbonate of soda
¼ cup soft light-brown sugar
pinch of salt
¼ cup treacle
60 g butter
2 tablespoons finely chopped glacé ginger
1 egg
¼ cup buttermilk

TOPPING
1 cup icing sugar
1 tablespoon water
glacé ginger

Preheat the oven to 180°C and lightly grease a muffin tray. Mix the flour, baking powder, bicarbonate of soda, light-brown sugar and salt in a bowl. In a saucepan, cook the treacle and butter over a gentle heat until melted, mixing well, then stir in the glacé ginger. In another bowl, gently beat the egg, then beat in the treacle mixture with the buttermilk. Pour the wet ingredients into the flour mixture and mix lightly until just combined. Spoon the batter into the prepared muffin tray.

Bake for 25–30 minutes or until the muffins spring back when lightly pressed. Remove the muffins from the oven and turn them out onto a wire rack to cool.

To make the topping, mix the icing sugar and water in a bowl. Drizzle 1 tablespoon icing over each cool muffin, then decorate them with a little glacé ginger.

Orange and Chocolate Muffins

2 cups unbleached self-raising flour
grated zest of 1 orange
¾ cup soft light-brown sugar
60 g dark chocolate, finely grated
½ cup dark Choc Bits
2 eggs
½ cup sour cream
125 g butter, melted
½ cup fresh orange juice

Preheat the oven to 180°C and lightly grease a muffin tray. Mix the flour, orange zest, light-brown sugar, grated chocolate and Choc Bits in a bowl. In a separate bowl, lightly whisk the eggs with the sour cream, melted butter and orange juice. Pour the wet ingredients into the flour mixture and mix lightly until just combined. Spoon the batter into the prepared muffin tray.

Bake for 25–30 minutes or until the muffins spring back when lightly pressed. Remove the muffins from the oven and turn them out onto a wire rack to cool.

Pear and Gingerbread Muffins

2 cups plain flour
½ teaspoon bicarbonate of soda
½ cup soft light-brown sugar
1 heaped teaspoon ground ginger
1 cup instant oats
½ cup treacle
½ cup butter
2 eggs
1 cup roughly chopped canned pear

Preheat the oven to 180°C and lightly grease a muffin tray. Mix the flour, bicarbonate of soda, light-brown sugar, ginger and instant oats in a bowl. In a saucepan, cook the treacle and butter over a gentle heat until melted, mixing well. Remove the pan from the heat. In another bowl, gently beat the eggs, then beat in the treacle and butter mixture. Pour the wet ingredients into the flour mixture and mix lightly until just combined, then fold in the pear. Spoon the batter into the prepared muffin tray.

Bake for 25–30 minutes or until the muffins spring back when lightly pressed. Remove the muffins from the oven and turn them out onto a wire rack to cool.

Pecan Polenta Muffins with Maple Syrup

1½ cups unbleached self-raising flour
½ cup coarse polenta
2 tablespoons soft light-brown sugar
1 cup pecan nuts, chopped
2 eggs
¾ cup buttermilk
80 g butter, melted
⅓ cup maple syrup

Preheat the oven to 180°C and lightly grease a muffin tray. Mix the flour, polenta, light-brown sugar and pecans in a bowl. In a separate bowl, lightly whisk the eggs with the buttermilk, melted butter and maple syrup. Pour the wet ingredients into the flour mixture and mix lightly until just combined. Spoon the batter into the prepared muffin tray.

Bake for 25–30 minutes or until the muffins spring back when lightly pressed. Remove the muffins from the oven and turn them out onto a wire rack to cool.

Pineapple Muffins

2 cups unbleached plain flour
2½ teaspoons baking powder
¾ cup castor sugar
2 eggs
125 g butter, melted
¾ cup pineapple juice
1 teaspoon vanilla essence
½ cup finely chopped fresh pineapple

Preheat the oven to 180°C and lightly grease a muffin tray. Mix the flour, baking powder and castor sugar in a bowl. In a separate bowl, lightly whisk the eggs with the butter, vanilla essence and pineapple juice. Pour the wet ingredients into the flour mixture and mix lightly until just combined. Fold in the fresh pineapple. Spoon the batter into the prepared muffin tray.

Bake for 25–30 minutes or until the muffins spring back when lightly pressed. Remove the muffins from the oven and turn them out onto a wire rack to cool.

Rainbow Muffins

2 cups unbleached self-raising flour
¾ cup castor sugar
⅓ cup hundreds and thousands
2 eggs
1 cup buttermilk
60 g butter, melted

Preheat the oven to 180°C and lightly grease a muffin tray. Mix the flour, castor sugar and hundreds and thousands in a bowl. In a separate bowl, lightly whisk the eggs with the buttermilk and melted butter. Pour the wet ingredients into the flour mixture and mix lightly until just combined. Spoon the batter into the prepared muffin tray.

Bake for 25–30 minutes or until the muffins spring back when lightly pressed. Remove the muffins from the oven and turn them out onto a wire rack to cool.

Roasted Pecan and Treacle Muffins

1 cup unbleached self-raising flour
2 cups wholemeal self-raising flour
¾ cup soft light-brown sugar
1 cup dry-roasted pecan nuts, chopped
1 tablespoon grated orange zest
¾ cup hot water
½ cup treacle
¼ cup milk

Preheat the oven to 150°C and lightly grease a muffin tray. Mix the flours with the light-brown sugar, pecans and orange zest in a bowl. In a separate bowl, lightly whisk the hot water with the treacle, then stir in the milk thoroughly. Pour the wet ingredients into the flour mixture and mix lightly until just combined. Spoon the batter into the prepared muffin tray.

Bake for 45–55 minutes or until the muffins spring back when lightly pressed. Remove the muffins from the oven and turn them out onto a wire rack to cool.

Sesame Seed Muffins

2 cups unbleached self-raising flour
⅓ cup castor sugar
⅓ cup soft light-brown sugar
⅓ cup toasted sesame seeds
1 egg
1¼ cups buttermilk
80 g butter, melted
1 tablespoon sesame oil

Preheat the oven to 180°C and lightly grease a muffin tray. Mix the flour, sugars and sesame seeds in a bowl. In a separate bowl, lightly whisk the egg with the buttermilk, melted butter and sesame oil. Pour the wet ingredients into the flour mixture and mix lightly until just combined. Spoon the batter into the prepared muffin tray.

Bake for 25–30 minutes or until the muffins spring back when lightly pressed. Remove the muffins from the oven and turn them out onto a wire rack to cool.

Spiced Pumpkin Muffins

2 cups unbleached self-raising flour
1 cup soft light-brown sugar
1 teaspoon ground cinnamon
½ teaspoon ground ginger
¼ teaspoon mixed spice
½ cup pecan nuts, chopped
2 eggs
1 cup buttermilk
¼ cup canola oil
1 cup mashed cooked pumpkin

Preheat the oven to 180°C and lightly grease a muffin tray. Mix the flour, light-brown sugar, spices and pecans in a bowl. In a separate bowl, lightly whisk the eggs with the buttermilk and canola oil, then stir in the mashed pumpkin. Pour the wet ingredients into the flour mixture and mix lightly until just combined. Spoon the batter into the prepared muffin tray.

Bake for 25–30 minutes or until the muffins

spring back when lightly pressed. Remove the muffins from the oven and turn them out onto a wire rack to cool.

Spicy Mandarin Muffins

2 cups unbleached plain flour
1 teaspoon baking powder
1 tablespoon ground cinnamon
½ teaspoon freshly grated nutmeg
1 teaspoon ground cardamom
3 eggs
1 cup castor sugar
1 cup canola oil
1 cup canned mandarin segments, drained and patted dry

Preheat the oven to 180°C and lightly grease a muffin tray. Mix the flour, baking powder and spices in a bowl. In a separate bowl, whisk the eggs and castor sugar until pale and thick, then add the canola oil in a slow stream, still whisking. Gently stir the wet ingredients into the flour mixture and then fold in the mandarin segments. Spoon the batter into the prepared muffin tray.

Bake for 25–30 minutes or until the muffins

spring back when lightly pressed. Remove the muffins from the oven and turn them out onto a wire rack to cool.

SAVOURY MUFFINS

Bacon and Creamy Corn Muffins

1 cup unbleached self-raising flour
1 cup coarse polenta
1 cup crumbled cooked bacon
pinch of salt
¼ teaspoon cayenne pepper
2 eggs
½ cup buttermilk
1 cup canned creamed sweetcorn
20 g butter, melted

Preheat the oven to 180°C and lightly grease a muffin tray. Mix the flour, polenta and bacon in a bowl and season with salt and cayenne pepper. In a separate bowl, lightly whisk the eggs with the buttermilk, creamed sweetcorn and melted butter. Pour the wet ingredients into the flour mixture and mix lightly until just combined. Spoon the batter into the prepared muffin tray.

Bake for 25–30 minutes or until the muffins spring back when lightly pressed. Remove the muffins from the oven and turn them out onto a wire rack to cool.

Basil, Feta and Spicy Sausage Muffins

2 cups unbleached self-raising flour
1 cup crumbled feta cheese
¼ cup shredded fresh basil
100 g finely chopped chorizo sausage
pinch of salt
freshly ground black pepper
2 eggs
1 cup buttermilk
80 g butter, melted

Preheat the oven to 180°C and lightly grease a muffin tray. Mix the flour, feta, basil, sausage, salt and pepper in a bowl. In a separate bowl, lightly whisk the eggs with the buttermilk and melted butter. Pour the wet ingredients into the flour mixture and mix lightly until just combined. Spoon the batter into the prepared muffin tray.

Bake for 25–30 minutes or until the muffins spring back when lightly pressed. Remove the muffins from the oven and turn them out onto a wire rack to cool.

Beer and Chilli Cheddar Muffins

2 cups unbleached self-raising flour
½ cup coarse polenta
1 tablespoon finely chopped chives
½ teaspoon cayenne pepper
1 cup finely grated tasty cheddar cheese
1–2 green chillies, seeded and finely chopped
2 eggs
40 g butter, melted
¾ cup beer

Preheat the oven to 180°C and lightly grease a muffin tray. Mix the flour, polenta, chives, cayenne pepper, cheddar and chilli in a bowl. In a separate bowl, lightly whisk the eggs with the melted butter, then stir in the beer. Pour the wet ingredients into the flour mixture and mix lightly until just combined. Spoon the batter into the prepared muffin tray.

Bake for 25–30 minutes or until the muffins spring back when lightly pressed. Remove the muffins from the oven and turn them out onto a wire rack to cool.

Blue Cheese, Walnut and Pear Muffins

2 cups unbleached self-raising flour
2 cups roughly grated pear
½ cup walnuts, finely chopped
½ teaspoon lemon pepper
2 eggs
¾ cup buttermilk
¼ cup canola oil
100 g soft blue cheese

Preheat the oven to 180°C and lightly grease a muffin tray. Mix the flour, pear, walnuts and lemon pepper in a bowl. In a separate bowl, lightly whisk the eggs with the buttermilk and canola oil. Pour the wet ingredients into the flour mixture and mix lightly until just combined. Spoon the batter into the prepared muffin tray. Push a piece of blue cheese into each muffin.

Bake for 25–30 minutes or until the muffins spring back when lightly pressed. Remove the muffins from the oven and turn them out onto a wire rack to cool.

Cheese and Mango Chutney Muffins

2 cups unbleached self-raising flour
1 cup finely grated tasty cheddar cheese
1 tablespoon finely chopped spring onion
1 teaspoon mustard powder
2 eggs
1 cup buttermilk
¼ cup canola oil
½ cup mango chutney

Preheat the oven to 180°C and lightly grease a muffin tray. Mix the flour, cheddar, spring onion and mustard powder in a bowl. In a separate bowl, lightly whisk the eggs with the buttermilk and canola oil, then stir in the mango chutney. Pour the wet ingredients into the flour mixture and mix lightly until just combined. Spoon the batter into the prepared muffin tray.

Bake for 25–30 minutes or until the muffins spring back when lightly pressed. Remove the muffins from the oven and turn them out onto a wire rack to cool.

Cheese, Corn and Rice Muffins

1 cup unbleached self-raising flour
¾ cup coarse polenta
½ cup cooked rice
½ cup finely grated cheddar cheese
¼ teaspoon cayenne pepper
½ teaspoon salt
2 eggs
1 cup buttermilk
80 g butter, melted

Preheat the oven to 180°C and lightly grease a muffin tray. Mix the flour, polenta, rice, cheddar, cayenne pepper and salt in a bowl. In a separate bowl, lightly whisk the eggs with the buttermilk and melted butter. Pour the wet ingredients into the flour mixture and mix lightly until just combined. Spoon the batter into the prepared muffin tray.

Bake for 25–30 minutes or until the muffins spring back when lightly pressed. Remove the muffins from the oven and turn them out onto a wire rack to cool.

Cheese, Onion and Potato-topped Muffins

2 cups unbleached self-raising flour
1 teaspoon mustard powder
½ teaspoon lemon pepper
1 egg
1 cup buttermilk
80 g butter, melted

TOPPING
2 potatoes, cooked, peeled and thinly sliced
1 onion, thinly sliced
¼ cup freshly grated parmesan cheese
1 teaspoon freshly chopped rosemary
freshly ground black pepper

Preheat the oven to 200°C and lightly grease a muffin tray. Mix the flour, mustard powder and lemon pepper in a bowl. In a separate bowl, lightly whisk the egg with the buttermilk and melted butter. Pour the wet ingredients into the flour mixture and mix lightly until just combined. Spoon the batter into the prepared muffin tray. Press 2 slices of potato and an onion ring into the top of each muffin, then sprinkle over the parmesan, a little rosemary and some pepper.

Bake for 25–30 minutes or until the muffins spring back when lightly pressed. Remove the muffins from the oven and turn them out onto a wire rack to cool.

Creamy Corn and Cheddar Muffins

1½ cups unbleached self-raising flour
½ cup coarse polenta
½ teaspoon mustard powder
½ teaspoon salt
1 cup finely grated tasty cheddar cheese
2 eggs
½ cup plain yoghurt
⅓ cup canola oil
1 cup canned creamed sweetcorn

Preheat the oven to 180°C and lightly grease a muffin tray. Mix the flour, polenta, mustard powder and salt in a bowl, then stir in the cheddar. In a separate bowl, lightly whisk the eggs with the yoghurt and canola oil, then stir in the creamed sweetcorn. Pour the wet ingredients into the flour mixture and mix lightly until just combined. Spoon the batter into the prepared muffin tray.

Bake for 25–30 minutes or until the muffins spring back when lightly pressed. Remove the muffins from the oven and turn them out onto a wire rack to cool.

Feta and Olive Muffins

2 cups unbleached self-raising flour
1 cup crumbled feta cheese
1 tablespoon finely chopped fresh basil
1 teaspoon dried rosemary
½ teaspoon freshly ground black pepper
1 egg
1 cup milk
80 g butter, melted
2 tablespoons roughly chopped kalamata olives

Preheat the oven to 180°C and lightly grease a muffin tray. Put the flour and feta in a bowl, then crumble the cheese through the flour with your fingers. Add the herbs and pepper. In a separate bowl, lightly whisk the egg with the milk and melted butter, then stir in the olives. Pour the wet ingredients into the flour mixture and mix lightly until just combined. Spoon the batter into the prepared muffin tray.

Bake for 25–30 minutes or until the muffins

spring back when lightly pressed. Remove the muffins from the oven and turn them out onto a wire rack to cool.

Feta and Potato Muffins

1 cup unbleached self-raising flour
1 cup wholemeal self-raising flour
250 g new small potatoes, cooked and roughly chopped
100 g feta cheese
2 tablespoons freshly chopped garlic chives
¼ teaspoon freshly ground black pepper
2 eggs
1 cup buttermilk
¼ cup canola oil

Preheat the oven to 180°C and lightly grease a muffin tray. Mix the flours, then stir in the potato and feta with your hands, crumbling both as you go, and add the garlic chives and pepper. In a separate bowl, lightly whisk the eggs with the buttermilk and canola oil. Pour the wet ingredients into the flour mixture and mix lightly until just combined. Spoon the batter into the prepared muffin tray.

Bake for 25–30 minutes or until the muffins spring back when lightly pressed. Remove the muffins from the oven and turn them out onto a wire rack to cool.

Fresh Herb Muffins

1 cup unbleached self-raising flour
1 cup wholemeal self-raising flour
⅓ cup freshly chopped herbs (chives, parsley, thyme, sage, basil, dill)
½ teaspoon lemon pepper
1 egg
1 cup buttermilk
125 g butter, melted

Preheat the oven to 180°C and lightly grease a muffin tray. Mix the flours, herbs and lemon pepper in a bowl. In a separate bowl, lightly whisk the egg with the buttermilk and melted butter. Pour the wet ingredients into the flour mixture and mix lightly until just combined. Spoon the batter into the prepared muffin tray.

Bake for 25–30 minutes or until the muffins spring back when lightly pressed. Remove the muffins from the oven and turn them out onto a wire rack to cool.

Fresh Sweetcorn and Chilli Muffins

1½ cups unbleached self-raising flour
½ cup coarse polenta
1 cup fresh corn kernels
¼ cup freshly grated parmesan cheese
2 eggs
1 cup buttermilk
½ cup canola oil
2 teaspoons chilli paste

Preheat the oven to 180°C and lightly grease a muffin tray. Mix the flour, polenta, corn and parmesan in a bowl. In a separate bowl, lightly whisk the eggs with the buttermilk, canola oil and chilli paste. Pour the wet ingredients into the flour mixture and mix lightly until just combined. Spoon the batter into the prepared muffin tray.

Bake for 25–30 minutes or until the muffins spring back when lightly pressed. Remove the muffins from the oven and turn them out onto a wire rack to cool.

Fresh Sweetcorn and Spring Onion Muffins

2 cups unbleached self-raising flour
1 cup fresh corn kernels
1 cup finely chopped spring onion
1 tablespoon freshly chopped dill
pinch of salt
freshly ground black pepper
2 eggs
½ cup canola oil
1 cup sour cream

Preheat the oven to 180°C and lightly grease a muffin tray. Mix the flour, corn, spring onion and dill in a bowl, then season with salt and pepper. In a separate bowl, lightly whisk the eggs with the canola oil and sour cream. Pour the wet ingredients into the flour mixture and mix lightly until just combined. Spoon the batter into the prepared muffin tray.

Bake for 25–30 minutes or until the muffins

spring back when lightly pressed. Remove the muffins from the oven and turn them out onto a wire rack to cool. Serve with slices of smoked salmon.

FOR A DELICIOUS BUTTER TO SERVE WITH SAVOURY MUFFINS, CREAM 100 g SOFTENED BUTTER WITH 1 TEASPOON DIJON MUSTARD, 2 TABLESPOONS FRESHLY CHOPPED BASIL, 1 TABLESPOON FRESHLY CHOPPED PARSLEY AND 1 TABLESPOON FRESHLY CHOPPED CHIVES. CHILL UNTIL READY TO SERVE.

Ham and Mustard Muffins

1 cup unbleached self-raising flour
1 cup wholemeal self-raising flour
140 g leg ham, finely chopped
½ cup grated tasty cheddar cheese
1 egg
1 cup buttermilk
½ cup canola oil
2 tablespoons grainy mustard

Preheat the oven to 180°C and lightly grease a muffin tray. Mix the flours, ham and cheddar in a bowl. In a separate bowl, lightly whisk the egg with the buttermilk, canola oil and mustard. Pour the wet ingredients into the flour mixture and mix lightly until just combined. Spoon the batter into the prepared muffin tray.

Bake for 25–30 minutes or until the muffins spring back when lightly pressed. Remove the muffins from the oven and turn them out onto a wire rack to cool.

Herbed Feta and Onion Muffins

1 tablespoon olive oil
1 cup finely chopped onion
1 cup feta cheese
1 tablespoon finely chopped fresh sage
1 tablespoon finely chopped fresh chives
1 tablespoon finely chopped fresh parsley
2 cups unbleached self-raising flour
½ teaspoon freshly ground black pepper
2 eggs
1 cup buttermilk
⅓ cup light olive oil

Preheat the oven to 180°C and lightly grease a muffin tray. In a frying pan, heat the 1 tablespoon olive oil and cook the onion until lightly browned. Set aside to cool. Crumble the feta into a bowl, then stir in the fresh herbs to coat and mix in the flour and pepper. In a separate bowl, lightly whisk the eggs with the buttermilk and light olive oil, then stir in the cooked onion. Pour the wet ingredients into the flour mixture and mix lightly until just combined. Spoon the batter into the prepared muffin tray.

Bake for 25–30 minutes or until the muffins spring back when lightly pressed. Remove the muffins from the oven and turn them out onto a wire rack to cool.

WHEN PREPARING FRESH CHILLIES, WEAR RUBBER GLOVES TO PROTECT YOUR HANDS AND AVOID ANY FINGERS STRAYING NEAR EYES. THE 'HEAT' IS CONCENTRATED IN THE WHITE TISSUE AND THE SEEDS, SO DISCARD THESE BEFORE CHOPPING THE FLESH, IF YOU LIKE.

Leek and Bacon Muffins

2 teaspoons light olive oil
1 large leek, washed and thinly sliced
4 rashers rindless bacon, finely chopped
1½ cups unbleached self-raising flour
½ cup wholemeal self-raising flour
1 teaspoon paprika
2 eggs
1 cup buttermilk
⅓ cup light olive oil

Preheat the oven to 180°C and lightly grease a muffin tray. Heat the 2 teaspoons olive oil in a frying pan and sauté the leek until lightly browned. Add the bacon and cook for a further 2–3 minutes. Remove the pan from the heat and allow to cool slightly. Mix the flours and paprika in a bowl. In a separate bowl, lightly whisk the eggs with the buttermilk and olive oil, then stir in the leek and bacon. Pour the wet ingredients into the flour mixture and mix lightly until just combined. Spoon the batter into the prepared muffin tray.

Bake for 25–30 minutes or until the muffins spring back when lightly pressed. Remove the muffins from the oven and turn them out onto a wire rack to cool.

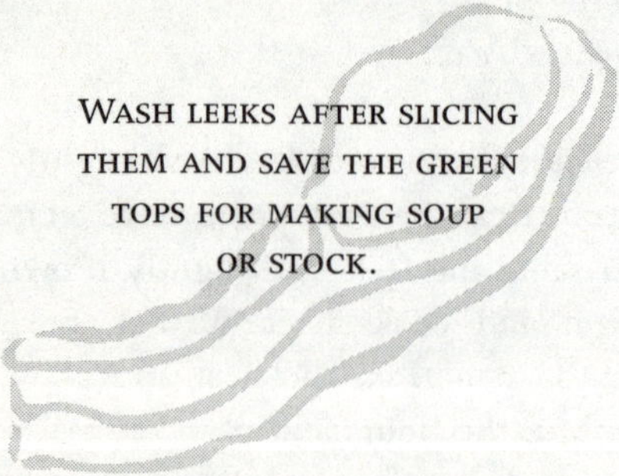

WASH LEEKS AFTER SLICING THEM AND SAVE THE GREEN TOPS FOR MAKING SOUP OR STOCK.

Mexican Chilli Pepper Corn Muffins

1½ cups unbleached self-raising flour
¾ cup coarse polenta
¼ teaspoon cayenne pepper
1 cup grated mozzarella cheese
2 eggs
1 cup buttermilk
80 g butter, melted
1 cup fresh corn kernels
1 fresh jalapeno chilli, seeded and finely chopped
1 cup seeded and finely diced red pepper

Preheat the oven to 180°C and lightly grease a muffin tray. Mix the flour, polenta and cayenne pepper in a bowl, then stir in the mozzarella. In a separate bowl, lightly whisk the eggs with the buttermilk and melted butter, then stir in the corn, jalapeno chilli and red pepper. Pour the wet ingredients into the flour mixture and mix lightly until just combined. Spoon the batter into the prepared muffin tray.

Bake for 25–30 minutes or until the muffins spring back when lightly pressed. Remove the muffins from the oven and turn them out onto a wire rack to cool.

Mushroom and Cheddar Muffins

250 g mushrooms, wiped clean and thinly sliced
10 g butter
½ teaspoon dried thyme
1½ cups unbleached self-raising flour
½ cup wholemeal self-raising flour
1 cup grated cheddar cheese
1 tablespoon finely chopped fresh garlic chives
pinch of freshly ground black pepper
1 egg
¾ cup buttermilk
¼ cup canola oil

Preheat the oven to 180°C and lightly grease a muffin tray. Melt the butter in a frying pan and add the mushrooms and thyme. Cook for about 5 minutes until softened, then allow to cool. Mix the flours, cheese, garlic chives and pepper in a bowl. In a separate bowl, lightly whisk the egg with the buttermilk and canola oil, then stir in the mushrooms and their juices. Pour the wet ingredients into the flour mixture and mix lightly until just combined. Spoon the batter into the prepared muffin tray.

Bake for 25–30 minutes or until the muffins spring back when lightly pressed. Remove the muffins from the oven and turn them out onto a wire rack to cool.

Mushroom and Parmesan Polenta Muffins

1 cup unbleached self-raising flour
¾ cup coarse polenta
½ cup freshly grated parmesan cheese
¼ teaspoon cayenne pepper
1 cup finely chopped mushrooms
2 eggs
1 cup buttermilk
125 g butter, melted

Preheat the oven to 180°C and lightly grease a muffin tray. Mix the flour, polenta, parmesan and cayenne pepper in a bowl, then stir in the mushrooms. In a separate bowl, lightly whisk the eggs with the buttermilk and melted butter. Pour the wet ingredients into the flour mixture and mix lightly until just combined. Spoon the batter into the prepared muffin tray.

Bake for 25–30 minutes or until the muffins spring back when lightly pressed. Remove the muffins from the oven and turn them out onto a wire rack to cool.

Pesto and Sun-dried Tomato Muffins

2 cups unbleached self-raising flour
½ cup freshly grated parmesan cheese
¾ cup finely chopped sun-dried tomatoes
2 eggs
1 cup buttermilk
½ cup light olive oil
2 tablespoons pesto sauce

Preheat the oven to 180°C and lightly grease a muffin tray. Mix the flour, parmesan and sun-dried tomatoes in a bowl. In a separate bowl, lightly whisk the eggs with the buttermilk, olive oil and pesto. Pour the wet ingredients into the flour mixture and mix lightly until just combined. Spoon the batter into the prepared muffin tray.

Bake for 25–30 minutes or until the muffins spring back when lightly pressed. Remove the muffins from the oven and turn them out onto a wire rack to cool.

Provolone, Carrot and Zucchini Muffins

2 cups unbleached self-raising flour
½ cup grated provolone cheese
1 cup peeled and finely grated carrot
1 cup finely grated zucchini
pinch of salt
¼ teaspoon freshly ground black pepper
2 eggs
1 cup buttermilk
½ cup canola oil
12 sun-dried tomatoes, roughly chopped

Preheat the oven to 180°C and lightly grease a muffin tray. Mix the flour, provolone, carrot, zucchini, salt and pepper in a bowl. In a separate bowl, lightly whisk the eggs with the buttermilk and canola oil. Pour the wet ingredients into the flour mixture and mix lightly until just combined. Spoon the batter into the prepared muffin tray. Sprinkle the chopped sun-dried tomatoes over the top of each muffin.

Bake for 25–30 minutes or until the muffins spring back when lightly pressed. Remove the muffins from the oven and turn them out onto a wire rack to cool.

Ricotta, Spinach and Parmesan Muffins

2 cups unbleached self-raising flour
1 cup freshly grated parmesan cheese
1½ cups finely shredded baby spinach leaves
1 teaspoon finely chopped fresh garlic chives
freshly ground black pepper
2 eggs
½ cup buttermilk
¼ cup canola oil
½ cup ricotta cheese

Preheat the oven to 180°C and lightly grease a muffin tray. Mix the flour, parmesan, spinach, garlic chives and pepper in a bowl. In a separate bowl, lightly whisk the eggs with the buttermilk, canola oil and ricotta. Pour the wet ingredients into the flour mixture and mix lightly until just combined. Spoon the batter into the prepared muffin tray.

Bake for 25–30 minutes or until the muffins spring back when lightly pressed. Remove the muffins from the oven and turn them out onto a wire rack to cool.

Ricotta and Zucchini Muffins

1 cup unbleached self-raising flour
1 cup wholemeal self-raising flour
1 tablespoon freshly chopped dill
1 cup finely grated zucchini
½ teaspoon freshly ground black pepper
2 eggs
1 cup ricotta cheese
125 g butter, melted

Preheat the oven to 180°C and lightly grease a muffin tray. Mix the flours, dill, zucchini and pepper in a bowl. In a separate bowl, lightly whisk the eggs with the ricotta and melted butter. Pour the wet ingredients into the flour mixture and mix lightly until just combined. Spoon the batter into the prepared muffin tray.

Bake for 25–30 minutes or until the muffins spring back when lightly pressed. Remove the muffins from the oven and turn them out onto a wire rack to cool.

Roasted Red Pepper and Brie Muffins

2 cups unbleached self-raising flour
¼ teaspoon cayenne pepper
1 tablespoon finely chopped fresh parsley
¾ cup roughly chopped roasted red pepper
¼ cup finely chopped spring onion
2 eggs
1 cup buttermilk
¼ cup light olive oil
80 g brie cheese

Preheat the oven to 180°C and lightly grease a muffin tray. Mix the flour, cayenne pepper, parsley, roasted red pepper and spring onion in a bowl. In a separate bowl, lightly whisk the eggs with the buttermilk and olive oil. Pour the wet ingredients into the flour mixture and mix lightly until just combined. Spoon the batter into the prepared muffin tray. Gently press a piece of brie into each muffin.

Bake for 25–30 minutes or until the muffins

spring back when lightly pressed. Remove the muffins from the oven and turn them out onto a wire rack to cool.

Roast halved and seeded peppers in a hot oven or under a griller until blackened. Transfer to a plastic bag to cool, then peel away the skin.

Salami and Green Olive Muffins

2 cups unbleached self-raising flour
¼ cup freshly grated parmesan cheese
½ teaspoon cayenne pepper
1 cup chopped mild salami
2 eggs
1 cup buttermilk
¼ cup light olive oil
½ cup finely chopped stuffed green olives

Preheat the oven to 180°C and lightly grease a muffin tray. Mix the flour, parmesan, cayenne pepper and salami in a bowl. In a separate bowl, lightly whisk the eggs with the buttermilk and olive oil, then stir in the olives. Pour the wet ingredients into the flour mixture and mix lightly until just combined. Spoon the batter into the prepared muffin tray.

Bake for 25–30 minutes or until the muffins spring back when lightly pressed. Remove the muffins from the oven and turn them out onto a wire rack to cool.

Spicy Vegetable Muffins

2 cups unbleached self-raising flour
1 teaspoon ground cumin
1 tablespoon finely chopped fresh coriander
2 tablespoons finely chopped spring onion
½ cup finely grated peeled carrot
½ cup finely grated zucchini
1 green chilli, seeded and finely chopped
½ teaspoon turmeric
2 eggs
1 cup buttermilk
50 g butter, melted

Preheat the oven to 180°C and lightly grease a muffin tray. Mix the flour, cumin, coriander, spring onion, carrot, zucchini and chilli in a bowl. Melt the butter in a saucepan with the turmeric. In a separate bowl, lightly whisk the eggs with the buttermilk and melted butter. Pour the wet ingredients into the flour mixture and mix lightly until just combined. Spoon the batter into the prepared muffin tray.

Bake for 25–30 minutes or until the muffins spring back when lightly pressed. Remove the muffins from the oven and turn them out onto a wire rack to cool. Serve with fruit chutney.

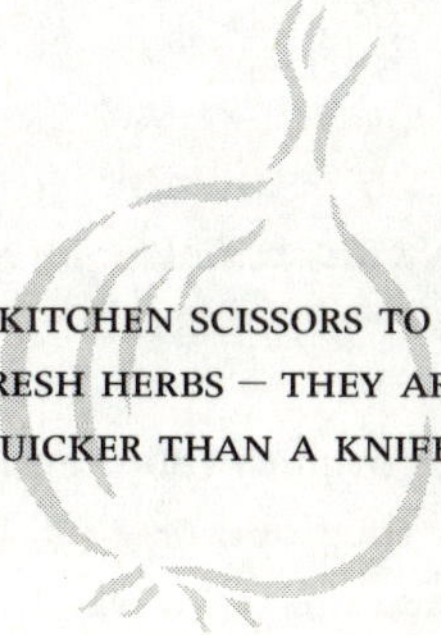

USE KITCHEN SCISSORS TO SNIP FRESH HERBS – THEY ARE QUICKER THAN A KNIFE.

Sun-dried Tomato, Feta and Polenta Muffins

1½ cups unbleached self-raising flour
½ cup coarse polenta
¾ cup roughly chopped feta cheese
¼ teaspoon cayenne pepper
½ teaspoon freshly ground black pepper
1 egg
1 cup buttermilk
½ cup canola oil
1 tablespoon finely chopped black olives
¾ cup roughly chopped sun-dried tomatoes

Preheat the oven to 180°C and lightly grease a muffin tray. Mix the flour, polenta, feta and peppers in a bowl. In a separate bowl, whisk the egg with the buttermilk and canola oil, then stir in the olives and sun-dried tomatoes. Pour the wet ingredients into the flour mixture and mix lightly until just combined. Spoon the batter into the prepared muffin tray.

Bake for 25–30 minutes or until the muffins spring back when lightly pressed. Remove the muffins from the oven and turn them out onto a wire rack to cool.

Three-cheese Muffins

2 cups unbleached self-raising flour
½ cup freshly grated parmesan cheese
½ cup roughly chopped feta cheese
2 tablespoons finely chopped fresh herbs
pinch of salt
½ teaspoon freshly ground black pepper
2 eggs
¾ cup buttermilk
½ cup ricotta cheese
60 g butter, melted

Preheat the oven to 180°C and lightly grease a muffin tray. Mix the flour, parmesan, feta, herbs, salt and pepper in a bowl. In a separate bowl, lightly whisk the eggs with the buttermilk, ricotta and melted butter. Pour the wet ingredients into the flour mixture and mix lightly stir until just combined. Spoon the batter into the prepared muffin tray.

Bake for 25–30 minutes or until the muffins spring back when lightly pressed. Remove the muffins from the oven and turn them out onto a wire rack to cool.

Vegetable-topped Cheese Muffins

1 cup unbleached self-raising flour
1 cup wholemeal self-raising flour
½ cup freshly grated parmesan cheese
2 eggs
1 cup buttermilk
¼ cup canola oil

TOPPING
2 tablespoons olive oil
1 small Spanish onion, peeled and sliced into rings
1 small red pepper, seeded and julienned
1 zucchini, coarsely grated
1 clove garlic, finely chopped
2 Roma tomatoes, roughly chopped
½ teaspoon freshly ground black pepper

Preheat the oven to 180°C and lightly grease a muffin tray. To make the topping, gently heat the oil in a frying pan and sauté the vegetables until softened. Remove the pan from the heat and set aside to cool.

Mix the flours and parmesan in a bowl. In a separate bowl, lightly whisk the eggs with the buttermilk and canola oil. Pour the wet ingredients into the flour mixture and mix lightly until just combined. Spoon the batter into the prepared muffin tray, then press a little of the cooked vegetables into the top of each muffin.

Bake for 25–30 minutes or until the muffins spring back when lightly pressed. Remove the muffins from the oven and turn them out onto a wire rack to cool.

SPECIAL SWEET TREATS

Banana, Macadamia Nut and Wattleseed Muffins

1 tablespoon wattleseeds
½ cup hot water
2 cups unbleached self-raising flour
¼ cup soft light-brown sugar
½ cup roughly chopped macadamia nuts
2 bananas, peeled and roughly chopped
2 eggs
¼ cup canola oil
½ cup buttermilk

Soak the wattleseeds in the hot water and allow to cool. Preheat the oven to 180°C and lightly grease a muffin tray. Mix the flour, light-brown sugar, macadamia nuts and banana in a bowl. In a separate bowl, lightly whisk the eggs with the buttermilk, canola oil and wattleseeds and their soaking water. Pour the wet ingredients into the flour mixture and mix lightly until just combined. Spoon the batter into the prepared muffin tray.

Bake for 25–30 minutes or until the muffins spring back when lightly pressed. Remove the muffins from the oven and turn them out onto a wire rack to cool.

NATIVE WATTLESEEDS ARE AVAILABLE FROM MOST GOOD DELICATESSENS. STRONG BLACK COFFEE CAN BE SUBSTITUTED SUCCESSFULLY FOR THE WATTLESEEDS AND THEIR SOAKING WATER, HOWEVER.

Banana Muffins with Passionfruit Lime Syrup

2 cups unbleached self-raising flour
½ cup soft light-brown sugar
3 bananas, roughly chopped
2 eggs
1 cup buttermilk
60 g butter, melted

PASSIONFRUIT LIME SYRUP
pulp of 4 passionfruit
juice of 2 limes
½ cup castor sugar

Preheat the oven to 180°C and lightly grease a muffin tray. Mix the flour, light-brown sugar and banana in a bowl. In a separate bowl, lightly whisk the eggs with the buttermilk and melted butter. Pour the wet ingredients into the flour mixture and mix lightly until just combined. Spoon the batter into the prepared muffin tray.

Bake for 25–30 minutes or until the muffins spring back when lightly pressed. While the muffins are cooking, make the passionfruit lime syrup. Put all the ingredients into a small saucepan and cook over a gentle heat, stirring, until the castor sugar has dissolved. Bring to a boil and cook for 6–8 minutes or until the syrup has reduced. Remove the pan from the heat and allow to cool. Remove the muffins from the oven and turn them out onto a wire rack. Pour a little of the syrup over each muffin. Serve warm.

Chocolate and Almond Sour Cream Muffins

1 cup unbleached self-raising flour
¼ cup cocoa powder
1 cup ground almonds
1 teaspoon instant coffee
1 cup Choc Bits
2 eggs
60 g butter, melted
¾ cup sour cream

Preheat the oven to 180°C and lightly grease a muffin tray. Mix the flour, ground almonds, cocoa powder, instant coffee and Choc Bits in a bowl. In a separate bowl, lightly whisk the eggs with the melted butter and sour cream. Pour the wet ingredients into the flour mixture and mix lightly until just combined. Spoon the batter into the prepared muffin tray.

Bake for 25–30 minutes or until the muffins spring back when lightly pressed. Remove the muffins from the oven and turn them out onto a wire rack to cool.

Chocolate Coffee Crumble Muffins

2 cups unbleached self-raising flour
¾ cup soft light-brown sugar
2 eggs
½ cup cold strong black coffee
½ cup light sour cream
½ cup canola oil

CRUMBLE
60 g dark cooking chocolate, chopped
¼ cup soft light-brown sugar
1 teaspoon grated orange zest
½ teaspoon ground cinnamon
½ teaspoon instant coffee
25 g chilled butter, diced

Preheat the oven to 180°C and lightly grease a muffin tray. In a food processor, blend the crumble ingredients for 15 seconds. Mix the flour and light-brown sugar in a bowl. In a separate bowl, lightly whisk the eggs with the coffee, sour cream and canola oil. Pour the wet ingredients into the flour mixture and mix lightly until just combined. Sprinkle the crumble mixture over the dough and using a round-bladed knife draw it into the mixture with four strokes to create a marbled effect. Spoon the batter into the prepared muffin tray.

Bake for 25–30 minutes or until the muffins spring back when lightly pressed. Remove the muffins from the oven and turn them out onto a wire rack to cool.

Chocolate Rum and Raisin Muffins

¼ cup dark rum
1 cup raisins
2 cups unbleached self-raising flour
½ cup soft light-brown sugar
¼ cup cocoa powder
½ teaspoon ground cinnamon
75 g dark chocolate, finely grated
2 eggs
1 cup buttermilk
60 g butter, melted

Heat the rum in a saucepan and soak the raisins off the heat for 30 minutes. Preheat the oven to 180°C and lightly grease a muffin tray. Mix the flour, light-brown sugar, cocoa powder, cinnamon and chocolate in a bowl. In a separate bowl, lightly whisk the eggs with the buttermilk and melted butter, then stir in the rum and raisins. Pour the wet ingredients into the flour mixture and mix lightly until just combined. Spoon the batter into the prepared muffin tray.

Bake for 25–30 minutes or until the muffins spring back when lightly pressed. Remove the muffins from the oven and turn them out onto a wire rack to cool.

Christmas Apple and Fruit Mince Muffins

2 cups unbleached self-raising flour
1 apple, peeled and grated
½ teaspoon ground cinnamon
½ teaspoon lemon zest
2 eggs
½ cup buttermilk
60 g butter, melted
2 tablespoons rum
¾ cup fruit mince

Preheat the oven to 180°C and lightly grease a muffin tray. Mix the flour, apple, cinnamon and lemon zest in a bowl. In a separate bowl, lightly whisk the eggs with the buttermilk, melted butter and rum. Pour the wet ingredients into the flour mixture and mix lightly until just combined, then stir in the fruit mince. Spoon the batter into the prepared muffin tray.

Bake for 25–30 minutes or until the muffins

spring back when lightly pressed. Remove the muffins from the oven and turn them out onto a wire rack to cool.

Christmas Fruit Muffins

2 cups unbleached self-raising flour
¼ cup castor sugar
1 teaspoon mixed spice
1 teaspoon ground cinnamon
1 cup mixed dried fruit
½ cup roughly chopped glacé cherries
¼ cup ground almonds
1 egg
1 cup milk
2 tablespoons brandy
60 g butter, melted

DECORATION
ready-to-roll white icing
sherry

Preheat the oven to 180°C and lightly grease a muffin tray. Mix the flour, castor sugar, spices, dried fruit, glacé cherries and ground almonds in a bowl. In a separate bowl, lightly whisk the egg with the milk, brandy and melted butter. Pour the wet ingredients into the flour mixture and mix lightly until just combined. Spoon the batter into the prepared muffin tray.

Bake for 25–30 minutes or until the muffins spring back when lightly pressed. Remove the muffins from the oven and turn them out onto a wire rack to cool. Roll out the white icing and cut out a star or holly leaf shape. Brush the top of each cooled muffin with sherry and decorate with the icing shape.

READY-TO-ROLL ICING CAN BE BOUGHT FROM SPECIALITY FOOD STORES AND SOME SUPERMARKETS.

Cinnamon Muffins

2 cups unbleached self-raising flour
½ cup castor sugar
¼ teaspoon freshly grated nutmeg
1 egg
¾ cup buttermilk
⅓ cup canola oil

COATING
180 g butter
½ cup castor sugar
1 teaspoon ground cinnamon

Preheat the oven to 180°C and lightly grease a muffin tray. Mix the flour, castor sugar and nutmeg in a bowl. In a separate bowl, lightly whisk the egg with the buttermilk and canola oil. Pour the wet ingredients into the flour mixture and mix lightly until just combined. Spoon the batter into the prepared muffin tray.

Bake for 25–30 minutes or until the muffins

spring back when lightly pressed. Remove the muffins from the oven and turn them out onto a wire rack to cool a little. In the meantime, make the coating. Melt the butter in a saucepan, then pour it into a large bowl. In a separate, shallow bowl, mix the castor sugar and cinnamon. Using tongs, dip one muffin at a time into the butter and then roll it in the cinnamon sugar. Continue until all the muffins have been coated. Serve immediately.

Coconut Lime Muffins

2 cups unbleached self-raising flour
½ cup castor sugar
½ cup desiccated coconut
1 teaspoon grated lime zest
2 eggs
½ cup buttermilk
½ cup coconut milk
80 g butter, melted
lime marmalade

Preheat the oven to 180°C and lightly grease a muffin tray. Mix the flour, castor sugar, coconut and lime zest in a bowl. In a separate bowl, lightly whisk the eggs with the buttermilk, coconut milk and melted butter. Pour the wet ingredients into the flour mixture and mix lightly until just combined. Spoon the batter into the prepared muffin tray. Spoon a little lime marmalade onto each muffin.

Bake for 25–30 minutes or until the muffins spring back when lightly pressed. Remove the muffins from the oven and turn them out onto a wire rack to cool.

Coconut and Mango Muffins

1½ cups unbleached self-raising flour
½ cup soft light-brown sugar
½ cup desiccated coconut
1 cup roughly chopped mango flesh
1 egg
1 cup buttermilk
80 g butter, melted

Preheat the oven to 180°C and lightly grease a muffin tray. Mix the flour, light brown sugar and coconut, then stir in the mango. In a separate bowl, lightly whisk the egg with the buttermilk and melted butter. Pour the wet ingredients into the flour mixture and mix lightly until just combined. Spoon the batter into the prepared muffin tray.

Bake for 25–30 minutes or until the muffins spring back when lightly pressed. Remove the muffins from the oven and turn them out onto a wire rack to cool.

Custard Apple and Glacé Pineapple Muffins

2 cups unbleached self-raising flour
¼ cup castor sugar
½ cup chopped glacé pineapple
½ teaspoon grated lemon zest
flesh of 1 large ripe custard apple
1 egg
1 cup buttermilk
80 g butter, melted

Preheat the oven to 180°C and lightly grease a muffin tray. Mix the flour, castor sugar, glacé pineapple and lemon zest in a bowl. In a food processor, blend the custard apple flesh with the egg, buttermilk and melted butter. Pour the wet ingredients into the flour mixture and mix lightly until just combined. Spoon the batter into the prepared muffin tray.

Bake for 25–30 minutes or until the muffins spring back when lightly pressed. Remove the muffins from the oven and turn them out onto a wire rack to cool.

Easter Hot Cross Muffins

2 cups unbleached self-raising flour
½ cup soft light-brown sugar
2 teaspoons ground cinnamon
2 teaspoons mixed spice
1 cup roughly chopped white chocolate buttons
2 eggs
1 cup buttermilk
⅓ cup canola oil

Preheat the oven to 180°C and lightly grease a muffin tray. Mix the flour, light-brown sugar, spices and half the white chocolate buttons in a bowl. In a separate bowl, lightly whisk the eggs with the buttermilk and canola oil. Pour the wet ingredients into the flour mixture and mix lightly until just combined. Spoon the batter into the prepared muffin tray.

Bake for 25–30 minutes or until the muffins spring back when lightly pressed. Remove the muffins from the oven and turn them out onto a wire rack to cool. Melt the remaining white chocolate buttons in a bowl over a saucepan of simmering water or in a microwave oven on High for 30 seconds. Using a piping bag, pipe a white cross on top of each warm muffin.

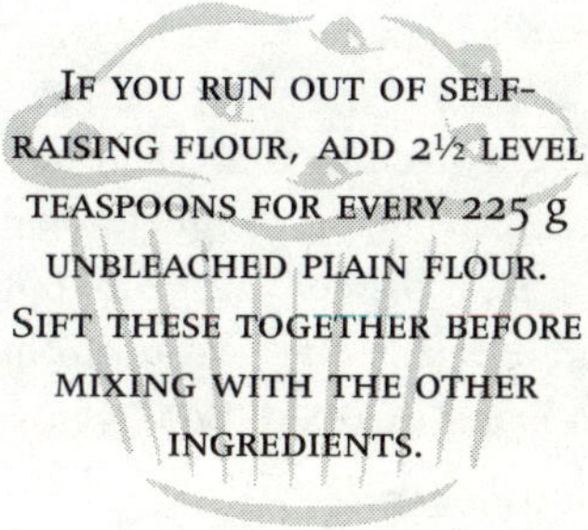

IF YOU RUN OUT OF SELF-RAISING FLOUR, ADD 2½ LEVEL TEASPOONS FOR EVERY 225 g UNBLEACHED PLAIN FLOUR. SIFT THESE TOGETHER BEFORE MIXING WITH THE OTHER INGREDIENTS.

Golden Fig Muffins

2 cups unbleached self-raising flour
¼ cup soft light-brown sugar
pinch of salt
¼ cup golden syrup
60 g butter
1 cup roughly chopped dried figs
2 eggs
½ cup buttermilk

Preheat the oven to 180°C and lightly grease a muffin tray. Mix the flour, light-brown sugar and salt in a bowl. Heat the golden syrup, butter and figs in a saucepan over a gentle heat until the butter has melted, then bring to a boil. Cook gently for 5 minutes until the figs have softened. Remove the pan from the heat and allow to cool. Add the eggs and buttermilk to the cooled mixture, and mix in thoroughly. Pour the wet ingredients into the flour mixture and mix lightly until just combined. Spoon the batter into the prepared muffin tray.

Bake for 20–25 minutes or until the muffins spring back when lightly pressed. Remove the muffins from the oven and turn them out onto a wire rack to cool.

Mixed Fruit and Sherry Muffins

1 cup mixed dried fruit
⅓ cup medium–dry sherry
½ cup soft light-brown sugar
75 g butter
2 cups unbleached self-raising flour
½ teaspoon ground cinnamon
¼ teaspoon mixed spice
2 eggs
1 cup buttermilk

Preheat the oven to 180°C and lightly grease a muffin tray. Heat the dried fruit, sherry, light-brown sugar and butter in a saucepan over a gentle heat, stirring, until the butter and sugar have melted. Remove the pan from the heat and allow to cool. Mix the flour and spices in a bowl. In a separate bowl, lightly whisk the eggs with the buttermilk, then stir in the cooled fruit mixture. Pour the wet ingredients into the flour mixture and lightly mix until just combined. Spoon the batter into the prepared muffin tray.

Bake for 25–30 minutes or until the muffins spring back when lightly pressed. Remove the muffins from the oven and turn them out onto a wire rack to cool.

Plum Streusel Muffins

1½ cups unbleached self-raising flour
½ cup wholemeal self-raising flour
⅓ cup soft light-brown sugar
1 cup roughly chopped plums
1 teaspoon grated lemon zest
2 eggs
80 g butter, melted
¾ cup plain yoghurt

STREUSEL
2 tablespoons unbleached plain flour
2 tablespoons soft light-brown sugar
½ teaspoon ground cinnamon
1 tablespoon finely chopped walnuts
25 g softened butter

Preheat the oven to 180°C and lightly grease a muffin tray. To make the streusel, put all the ingredients into a bowl, then rub the butter through with your fingers to make coarse crumbs. Mix the flours, light-brown sugar, plums and lemon zest in another bowl. In a separate bowl again, lightly whisk the eggs with the melted butter and yoghurt. Pour the wet ingredients into the flour mixture and mix lightly until just combined. Spoon the batter into the muffin tray, then sprinkle a little streusel over each muffin.

Bake for 25–30 minutes or until the muffins spring back when lightly pressed. Remove the muffins from the oven and turn them out on a wire rack to cool.

Raspberry and White Chocolate Muffins

2 cups unbleached self-raising flour
¼ cup castor sugar
200 g fresh or *frozen raspberries*
1 cup white chocolate buttons
1 egg
1 cup buttermilk
80 g butter, melted

Preheat the oven to 180°C and lightly grease a muffin tray. Mix the flour, castor sugar and raspberries in a bowl, then stir in the white chocolate buttons. In a separate bowl, lightly whisk the egg with the buttermilk and melted butter. Pour the wet ingredients into the flour mixture and mix lightly until just combined. Spoon the batter into the prepared muffin tray.

Bake for 25–30 minutes or until the muffins spring back when lightly pressed. Remove the muffins from the oven and turn them out onto a wire rack to cool.

Rhubarb and Amaretti Muffins

2 cups unbleached self-raising flour
2 tablespoons soft light-brown sugar
250 g rhubarb, roughly chopped
1 cup crushed amaretti biscuits
2 eggs
½ cup buttermilk
⅓ cup canola oil
¼ cup ricotta cheese

Preheat the oven to 180°C and lightly grease a muffin tray. Mix the flour, light-brown sugar, rhubarb and crushed amaretti biscuits in a bowl. In a separate bowl, lightly whisk the eggs with the buttermilk, canola oil and ricotta. Pour the wet ingredients into the flour mixture and mix lightly until just combined. Spoon the batter into the prepared muffin tray.

Bake for 25–30 minutes or until the muffins spring back when lightly pressed. Remove the muffins from the oven and turn them out onto a wire rack to cool.

Strawberry and Rhubarb Muffins

2 cups unbleached self-raising flour
½ cup soft light-brown sugar
½ teaspoon ground ginger
½ teaspoon ground cinnamon
250 g strawberries, hulled and roughly chopped
200 g rhubarb, trimmed and finely chopped
2 eggs
1 cup plain yoghurt
80 g butter, melted
¼ cup strawberry jam

Preheat the oven to 180°C and lightly grease a muffin tray. Mix the flour, light-brown sugar and spices in a bowl, then fold in the strawberries and rhubarb. In a separate bowl, lightly whisk the eggs with the yoghurt and melted butter. Pour the wet ingredients into the flour mixture and mix lightly until just combined. Spoon the batter into the prepared muffin tray. Dot a little strawberry jam on top of each muffin.

Bake for 25–30 minutes or until the muffins spring back when lightly pressed. Remove the muffins from the oven and turn them out onto a wire rack to cool.

LIGHT OF HAND
AND LIGHT ON SPEED!

Sweetcorn and Coconut Muffins

2 cups unbleached self-raising flour
1 cup castor sugar
2 eggs
80 g butter, melted
1 teaspoon vanilla essence
400 g drained canned corn kernels
1 cup coconut milk

Preheat the oven to 180°C and lightly grease a muffin tray. Mix the flour and castor sugar in a bowl. Blend the eggs with the melted butter, vanilla essence, corn and coconut milk in a food processor. Pour the wet ingredients into the flour mixture and mix lightly until just combined. Spoon the batter into the prepared muffin tray.

Bake for 40–50 minutes or until the muffins spring back when lightly pressed. Remove the muffins from the oven and turn them out onto a wire rack to cool.

RISE-AND-SHINE BREAKFAST MUFFINS

Banana and Peanut Butter Muffins

2 cups unbleached self-raising flour
1 cup soft light-brown sugar
3 bananas, roughly chopped
2 eggs
½ cup buttermilk
¼ cup canola oil
¾ cup crunchy peanut butter

Preheat the oven to 180°C and lightly grease a muffin tray. Mix the flour, light-brown sugar and banana in a bowl. In a separate bowl, lightly whisk the eggs with the buttermilk, canola oil and peanut butter. Pour the wet ingredients into the flour mixture and mix lightly until just combined. Spoon the batter into the prepared muffin tray.

Bake for 25–30 minutes or until the muffins spring back when lightly pressed. Remove the muffins from the oven and turn them out onto a wire rack to cool.

Breakfast Bran Refrigerator Muffins

1 cup water
4 cups All-Bran cereal
1 cup sultanas
2½ cups unbleached plain flour
1½ cups soft light-brown sugar
2 eggs
2 cups buttermilk
½ cup canola oil

Preheat the oven to 180°C and lightly grease a muffin tray. Bring the water to a boil in a saucepan, then remove from the heat and add the All-Bran and sultanas and set aside to cool. Mix the flour and light-brown sugar in a bowl. In a separate bowl, lightly whisk the eggs with the buttermilk and canola oil. Pour the wet ingredients into the flour mixture and mix lightly until just combined, then stir in the moistened cereal and sultanas. Refrigerate the mixture in an airtight container until ready to use. Spoon the batter into how ever many muffin cups you wish to cook at a time.

Bake for 25–30 minutes or until the muffins spring back when lightly pressed. Remove the muffins from the oven and turn them out onto a wire rack to cool.

THE UNCOOKED MUFFIN MIXTURE CAN BE KEPT FOR UP TO A WEEK IN THE REFRIGERATOR. MAKES ABOUT 24 × ⅓ CUP MUFFINS.

Breakfast Muesli Muffins

2 cups unbleached self-raising flour
½ cup soft light-brown sugar
1 cup natural muesli
2 eggs
1 cup plain yoghurt
⅓ cup canola oil

Preheat the oven to 180°C and lightly grease a muffin tray. Mix the flour, light-brown sugar and muesli in a bowl. In a separate bowl, lightly whisk the eggs with the yoghurt and canola oil. Pour the wet ingredients into the flour mixture and mix lightly until just combined. Spoon the batter into the prepared muffin tray.

Bake for 25–30 minutes or until the muffins spring back when lightly pressed. Remove the muffins from the oven and turn them out onto a wire rack to cool.

Lemon Blueberry Muffins

2 cups unbleached plain flour
1 teaspoon baking powder
¾ cup soft light-brown sugar
200 g fresh blueberries, washed
2 eggs
¼ cup buttermilk
½ cup vegetable oil
1 tablespoon grated lemon zest
1 teaspoon vanilla essence

Preheat the oven to 180°C and lightly grease a muffin tray. Mix the flour, baking powder, light-brown sugar and blueberries in a bowl. In a separate bowl, lightly whisk the eggs with the buttermilk, vegetable oil, lemon zest and vanilla essence. Pour the wet ingredients into the flour mixture and mix lightly until just combined. Spoon the batter into the prepared muffin tray.

Bake for 20–25 minutes or until the muffins spring back when lightly pressed. Remove the muffins from the oven and turn them out onto a wire rack to cool.

Marmalade Surprise Breakfast Muffins

1½ cups unbleached self-raising flour
½ cup soft light-brown sugar
½ cup oatbran
½ cup mixed candied peel
2 eggs
1 cup buttermilk
¼ cup canola oil
¼ cup orange marmalade

Preheat the oven to 180°C and lightly grease a muffin tray. Mix the flour, light-brown sugar, oatbran and candied peel in a bowl. In a separate bowl, lightly whisk the eggs with the buttermilk and canola oil. Pour the wet ingredients into the flour mixture and mix lightly until just combined. Spoon half the batter into the prepared muffin tray, then add 1 teaspoon of the orange marmalade to each muffin. Spoon in the remaining batter.

Bake for 25–30 minutes or until the muffins

spring back when lightly pressed. Remove the muffins from the oven and turn them out onto a wire rack to cool.

Oatbran, Apricot and Raisin Muffins

1½ cups unbleached self-raising flour
1 cup oatbran
¾ cup raisins
¾ cup roughly chopped dried apricots
2 tablespoons grated orange zest
2 tablespoons honey
2 tablespoons treacle
¼ cup canola oil
2 eggs
1 cup buttermilk

Preheat the oven to 180°C and lightly grease a muffin tray. Mix the flour, oatbran, raisins, apricots and orange zest in a bowl. Warm the honey and treacle with the canola oil in a saucepan, mixing well. In a separate bowl, lightly whisk the eggs with the buttermilk, then add the oil mixture. Pour the wet ingredients into the flour mixture and mix lightly until just combined. Spoon the batter into the prepared muffin tray.

Bake for 25–30 minutes or until the muffins spring back when lightly pressed. Remove the muffins from the oven and turn them out onto a wire rack to cool.

Oatbran, Walnut and Dried Fig Muffins

1 cup wholemeal self-raising flour
½ cup unbleached self-raising flour
½ cup soft light-brown sugar
½ cup oatbran
¾ cup finely chopped dried figs
¾ cup walnuts, roughly chopped
1 teaspoon finely grated lemon zest
1 egg
1 cup milk
¼ cup canola oil

Preheat the oven to 180°C and lightly grease a muffin tray. Mix the flours, light-brown sugar, oatbran, figs, walnuts and lemon zest in a bowl. In a separate bowl, lightly whisk the egg with the milk and canola oil. Pour the wet ingredients into the flour mixture and mix lightly until just combined. Spoon the batter into the prepared muffin tray.

Bake for 25–30 minutes or until the muffins

spring back when lightly pressed. Remove the muffins from the oven and turn them out onto a wire rack to cool.

Peanut Butter and Muesli Breakfast Muffins

1½ cups unbleached self-raising flour
½ cup soft light-brown sugar
1 teaspoon ground cinnamon
½ cup muesli
2 Granny Smith apples, peeled, cored and finely chopped
2 eggs
¾ cup buttermilk
¼ cup crunchy peanut butter

Preheat the oven to 180°C and lightly grease a muffin tray. Mix the flour, light-brown sugar, cinnamon, muesli and apple in a bowl. In a separate bowl, lightly whisk the eggs with the buttermilk and peanut butter. Pour the wet ingredients into the flour mixture and mix lightly until just combined. Spoon the batter into the prepared muffin tray.

Bake for 25–30 minutes or until the muffins spring back when lightly pressed. Remove the muffins from the oven and turn them out onto a wire rack to cool.

Rye, Polenta and Wheat Muffins

½ cup rye flour
1 cup wholemeal plain flour
½ cup coarse polenta
2 teaspoons baking powder
⅓ cup soft light-brown sugar
pinch of salt
1 cup sultanas
1 egg
1 cup buttermilk
⅓ cup canola oil
⅓ cup treacle

Preheat the oven to 180°C and lightly grease a muffin tray. Mix the flours, polenta, baking powder, light-brown sugar, salt and sultanas in a bowl. In a separate bowl, lightly whisk the egg with the buttermilk, canola oil and treacle. Pour the wet ingredients into the flour mixture and mix lightly until just combined. Spoon the batter into the prepared muffin tray.

Bake for 25–30 minutes or until the muffins spring back when lightly pressed. Remove the muffins from the oven and turn them out onto a wire rack to cool.

RYE FLOUR IS AVAILABLE FROM GOOD SUPERMARKETS AND HEALTH-FOOD STORES.

Strawberry and Orange Muffins

2 cups unbleached self-raising flour
⅓ cup soft light-brown sugar
200 g fresh strawberries, hulled and roughly chopped
2 eggs
¼ cup buttermilk
½ cup canola oil
1 teaspoon vanilla essence
⅓ cup orange marmalade

Preheat the oven to 180°C and lightly grease a muffin tray. Mix the flour and light-brown sugar in a bowl and stir in the strawberries. In a separate bowl, lightly whisk the eggs with the buttermilk, canola oil, vanilla essence and marmalade. Pour the wet ingredients into the flour mixture and mix lightly until just combined. Spoon the batter into the prepared muffin tray.

Bake for 20–25 minutes or until the muffins spring back when lightly pressed. Remove the muffins from the oven and turn them out onto a wire rack to cool.

Summer Berry Muffins

2 cups unbleached self-raising flour
½ cup soft light-brown sugar
2 cups mixed fresh berries (strawberries, blueberries, raspberries)
2 eggs
¼ cup buttermilk
½ cup vegetable oil
1 teaspoon vanilla essence
1 teaspoon grated lemon zest

Preheat the oven to 180°C and lightly grease a muffin tray. Mix the flour, light-brown sugar and berries in a bowl. In a separate bowl, lightly whisk the eggs with the buttermilk, vegetable oil, vanilla essence and lemon zest. Pour the wet ingredients into the flour mixture and mix lightly until just combined. Spoon the batter into the prepared muffin tray.

Bake for 20–25 minutes or until the muffins spring back when lightly pressed. Remove the muffins from the oven and turn them out onto a wire rack to cool.

Wheatgerm, Banana and Date Muffins

1 cup unbleached self-raising flour
1 cup wholemeal self-raising flour
½ cup soft light-brown sugar
½ cup wheatgerm
½ teaspoon ground cinnamon
½ cup chopped dates
1 egg
¼ cup yoghurt
¼ cup canola oil
2 cups mashed banana

Preheat the oven to 180°C and lightly grease a muffin tray. Mix the flours, light-brown sugar, wheatgerm, cinnamon and dates in a bowl. In a separate bowl, lightly whisk the egg with the yoghurt, canola oil and banana. Pour the wet ingredients into the flour mixture and mix lightly until just combined. Spoon the batter into the prepared muffin tray.

Bake for 25–30 minutes or until the muffins spring back when lightly pressed. Remove the muffins from the oven and turn them out onto a wire rack to cool.

Whole-orange Breakfast Muffins

1 cup wholemeal self-raising flour
2 cups oatbran
½ cup sultanas
1 thin-skinned orange, roughly chopped
1 ripe banana, roughly chopped
1 cup cold water
1 egg
25 g butter
1 tablespoon golden syrup

Preheat the oven to 180°C and lightly grease a muffin tray. Mix the flour, oatbran and sultanas in a bowl. In a food processor, blend the orange and banana until finely chopped, then add the water and egg. Melt the butter with the golden syrup in a saucepan, then stir this into the orange mixture. Pour the wet ingredients into the flour mixture and mix lightly until just combined. Spoon the batter into the prepared muffin tray.

Bake for 25–30 minutes or until the muffins

spring back when lightly pressed. Remove the muffins from the oven and turn them out onto a wire rack to cool.

Yoghurt and Honey Muffins

1 cup unbleached self-raising flour
1 cup wholemeal self-raising flour
2 tablespoons soft light-brown sugar
¼ cup rolled oats
¼ teaspoon ground cinnamon
¼ teaspoon ground nutmeg
1 egg
80 g butter, melted
1½ cups plain yoghurt
¼ cup honey

Preheat the oven to 180°C and lightly grease a muffin tray. Mix the flours, light-brown sugar, rolled oats and spices in a bowl. In a separate bowl, lightly whisk the egg with the melted butter, yoghurt and honey. Pour the wet ingredients into the flour mixture and mix lightly until just combined. Spoon the batter into the prepared muffin tray.

Bake for 25–30 minutes or until the muffins spring back when lightly pressed. Remove the muffins from the oven and turn them out onto a wire rack to cool.